DRAWN FROM NEW ENGLAND

DRAWN FROM NEW ENGLAND

Tasha Tudor

A Portrait In Words and Pictures By Bethany Tudor

COLLINS

Acknowledgements

The editor and William Collins Publishers, Incorporated herewith render thanks to the following authors, publishers, and photographers whose interest, cooperation and permission to reprint have made possible the preparation of this book. All possible care has been taken to trace the ownership of every selection or illustration included and to make full acknowledgement for its use. If any errors have accidentally occurred they will be corrected in subsequent editions, provided notification is sent to the publishers.

Rand McNally & Company for the illustration on page 67 from *A Time to Keep* by Tasha Tudor, copyright © 1977 by Tasha Tudor. Henry Z. Walck Inc./David McKay Inc. for the illustration on page 27 from *Pumpkin Moonshine* by Tasha Tudor, copyright © 1958 by Tasha Tudor (originally published in 1958 by Oxford University Press, New York); for the illustration on page 46 from *Alexander the Gander* by Tasha Tudor, copyright © 1939 by Tasha Tudor (originally published in 1939 by Oxford University Press, New York); and for the illustration on page 18 from *Snow Before Christmas* by Tasha Tudor, copyright © 1949 by Tasha Tudor (originally published in 1949 by Oxford University Press, New York). The Viking Press, for the illustration on page 64 from *Becky's Birthday*, by Tasha Tudor, copyright © 1947 by Tasha Tudor.

Irene Dash Greeting Cards Inc. for the cards illustrated by Tasha Tudor that appear on pages 30, 47, 60, 61, 64, 82, and 94. All copyright © by Tasha Tudor.

Linda Allen for the photographs on pages 68, 77 and 81; Bill Aller for the photograph on the jacket; Ann Beneduce for the photographs on the half-title page and on pages 14, 40, 49, 51, 73, 76, 78, 83, 87, 93 and 94; Bill Finney for the photographs on pages 89 and 96; Bill Lane for the photograph on page 90; Pete Main for the photograph on page 88; Pamela Sampson for the photograph on page 44; Marjorie Tudor for the photographs on the title page and on pages 84, 85, 92 and 93; Seth Tudor for the photographs on pages 85 and 91; Tasha Tudor for the photographs on pages 41, 45, 48, 50, 52, 58, 59, 63, 64, 65, 73, 74, 77, 78, and 91; Thomas Tudor for the photographs on pages 31, 39, 50, 54, 58, 66, 86, 87, and 90.

Particular gratitude is due to Nell Dorr, lifetime friend and distinguished photographer, for the use of the pictures on pages 5, 21, 22, 24, 25, 28, 32, 34, 35, 36, 37, 38, 42, 43, 46, and 72.

And special thanks to photographer Schecter Lee for his color pictures on pages 23, 26, 27, 67, 70, 71, 75, and 79, and for his expert preparation of nearly all the other photographs in this book, many of which were old, faded and extremely delicate.

Library of Congress Cataloging in Publication Data

Tudor, Bethany.   Drawn from New England

1. Tudor, Tasha. 2. Illustrators —
United States — Biography. I. Title.
NC975.5.T82T82   741'.092'4 [B]   79-14230
ISBN 0-529-05531-7

Contents

Books Illustrated by Tasha Tudor

Arranged Chronologically by Date of Publication

Pumpkin Moonshine. Written and illustrated by Tasha Tudor. Oxford University Press, New York, 1938. (This edition out-of-print, but story is available in **A Tasha Tudor Sampler,** see below).

Alexander the Gander. Written and illustrated by Tasha Tudor. Oxford University Press, New York, 1939. (Out-of-print).

The County Fair. Written and illustrated by Tasha Tudor. Oxford University Press, New York, 1940. (Now published by Henry Z. Walck/David McKay).

Snow Before Christmas. Written and illustrated by Tasha Tudor. Oxford University Press, New York, 1941. (Out-of-print).

A Tale for Easter. Written and illustrated by Tasha Tudor. Oxford University Press, New York, 1941. (Now published by Henry Z. Walck/David McKay).

Dorcas Porkus. Written and illustrated by Tasha Tudor. Oxford University Press, London, New York, Toronto, 1942. (Out-of-print).

The White Goose. Written and illustrated by Tasha Tudor. Farrar and Rinehart, Inc. Distributed by Oxford University Press, New York, 1943. (Out-of-print).

Mother Goose. Illustrated by Tasha Tudor. Henry Z. Walck, Inc., 1944. (Now Henry Z. Walck/David McKay).

Fairy Tales from Hans Christian Andersen. Illustrated by Tasha Tudor. Oxford University Press, New York, 1945. (Out-of-print).

Linsey Woolsey. Written and illustrated by Tasha Tudor. Oxford University Press, New York, 1946. (Out-of-print).

A Child's Garden of Verses by Robert Louis Stevenson. Illustrated by Tasha Tudor. Oxford University Press, New York, 1947. (Now published by Henry Z. Walck/David McKay).

The Dolls' House by Rumer Godden. Illustrated by Tasha Tudor. Georgian Webb Offset, Garden City, New York, 1947.

Jackanapes by Juliana Horatia Ewing. Illustrated by Tasha Tudor. Oxford University Press, New York, 1948. (Now published by Henry Z. Walck/David McKay).

Thistly B. Written and illustrated by Tasha Tudor. Oxford University Press, New York, 1949. (Out-of-print).

The Dolls' Christmas. Written and illustrated by Tasha Tudor. Henry Z. Walck, Inc., 1950. (Now Henry Z. Walck/David McKay).

Amanda and the Bear. Written and illustrated by Tasha Tudor. Oxford University Press, New York, 1951. (Out-of-print).

First Prayers. Illustrated by Tasha Tudor. Oxford University Press, New York, 1952. (Now Henry Z. Walck/David McKay).

Edgar Allen Crow. Written and illustrated by Tasha Tudor. Oxford University Press, New York, 1953. (Out-of-print).

A is for Annabelle. Written and illustrated by Tasha Tudor. Oxford University Press, New York, 1954. (Now published by Henry Z. Walck/David McKay).

Biggity Bantam by T.L. McCreedy, Jr. Illustrated by Tasha Tudor. Ariel Books, New York, 1954. (Out-of-print).

First Graces. Illustrated by Tasha Tudor. Oxford University Press, New York, 1955.

(Now published by Henry Z. Walck/David McKay).

Pekin White by T.L. McCready, Jr. Illustrated by Tasha Tudor. Ariel Books, New York, 1955. (Out-of-print).

Mr. Stubbs by T.L. McCready, Jr. Illustrated by Tasha Tudor. Ariel Books, New York, 1956. (Out-of-print).

1 is One. Written and illustrated by Tasha Tudor. Oxford University Press, New York, 1956.

Around the Year. Written and illustrated by Tasha Tudor. Henry Z. Walck, Inc., 1957. (Now Henry Z. Walck/David McKay).

And It Was So. Scriptural text selected and edited by Sara Klein Clarke. Illustrated by Tasha Tudor. The Westminster Press, Philadelphia, 1958. (Out-of-print).

Increase Rabbit by T.L. McCready, Jr. Illustrated by Tasha Tudor. Ariel Books, New York, 1958. (Out-of-print).

Adventures of a Beagle by T.L. McCready, Jr. Illustrated by Tasha Tudor. Ariel Books, New York, 1959. (Out-of-print).

The Lord Will Love Thee. Scriptural text selected and edited by Sara Klein Clarke. Illustrated by Tasha Tudor. The Westminster Press, 1959. (Out-of-print).

Becky's Birthday. Written and illustrated by Tasha Tudor. The Viking Press, New York, 1960. (Out-of-print).

My Brimful Book. Edited by Dana Bruce. Illustrated by Tasha Tudor and others. Platt and Munk Publishers, New York, 1961.

Becky's Christmas. Written and illustrated by Tasha Tudor. The Viking Press, New York, 1961.

The Tasha Tudor Book of Fairy Tales. Selected, edited and illustrated by Tasha Tudor. Platt and Munk Publishers, New York, 1961.

The Night Before Christmas by Clemente C. Moore. Illustrated by Tasha Tudor. Achille J. St. Onge, Worcester, 1962. (Out-of-print).

The Secret Garden by Frances Hodgson Burnett. Illustrated by Tasha Tudor. J.B. Lippincott Company, New York, Philadelphia, 1962.

A Little Princess by Frances Hodgson Burnett. Illustrated by Tasha Tudor. J.B. Lippincott Company, New York, Philadelphia, 1963.

A Round Dozen. Stories by Louisa May Alcott. Selected and with a Foreword by Anne Thaxter Eaton. Illustrated by Tasha Tudor. The Viking Press, New York, 1963. (Out-of-print).

Wings from the Wind. An anthology of poems selected and illustrated by Tasha Tudor. J.B. Lippincott Company, New York, Philadelphia, 1964.

Tasha Tudor's Favorite Stories. Illustrated by Tasha Tudor. J.B. Lippincott Company, New York, Philadelphia, 1965.

The Twenty-Third Psalm. Illustrated by Tasha Tudor. Achille J. St. Onge. Worcester, 1965. (Out-of-print).

First Delights. Written and illustrated by Tasha Tudor. Platt and Munk Publishers, New York, 1966. (Out-of-print).

Take Joy! The Tasha Tudor Christmas Book. Selected, edited, and illustrated by Tasha Tudor. The World Publishing Company, New York, Cleveland, 1966. (Now William Collins Publishers, Inc., New York, Cleveland).

The Wind in the Willows by Kenneth Grahame. Illustrated by Tasha Tudor. The World Publishing Company, New York, Cleveland, 1966. (Now William Collins Publishers, Inc., New York, Cleveland).

First Poems of Childhood. Illustrated by Tasha Tudor. Platt and Munk Publishers, New York, 1967.

More Prayers. Illustrated by Tasha Tudor. Henry Z. Walck, Inc., 1967. (Now Henry Z. Walck/David McKay).

The Real Diary of a Real Boy by Henry A. Shute. Illustrated by Tasha Tudor. Richard R. Smith Company, Inc., Noone House, Peterborough, New Hampshire, 1967. (Now published by William L. Bauhan, Inc., Dublin, N.H.)

Brite and Fair by Henry A. Shute. Illustrated by Tasha Tudor. Richard R. Smith Company, Inc., Noone House, Peterborough, New Hampshire, 1968. (Now published by William L. Bauhan, Inc., Dublin, N.H.)

New England Butt'ry Shelf Cookbook by Mary Mason Campbell. Illustrated by Tasha Tudor. The World Publishing Company, New York, Cleveland, 1968. (Out-of-print).

Little Women by Louisa May Alcott. Illustrated by Tasha Tudor. The World Publishing Company, New York, Cleveland, 1968.

New England Butt'ry Shelf Almanac by Mary Mason Campbell. Illustrated by Tasha Tudor. The World Publishing Company, New York, Cleveland, 1970. (Out-of-print).

Betty Crocker's Kitchen Gardens by Mary Mason Campbell. Illustrated by Tasha Tudor. The Golden Press, New York, 1971.

Corgiville Fair. Written and illustrated by Tasha Tudor. Thomas Y. Crowell Company, New York, 1971.

The Night Before Christmas by Clement C. Moore. Illustrated by Tasha Tudor. Rand McNally & Co., Chicago, 1975.

The Christmas Cat by Efner Tudor Holmes. Illustrated by Tasha Tudor. Thomas Y. Crowell Company, New York, 1976.

Amy's Goose by Efner Tudor Holmes. Illustrated by Tasha Tudor. Thomas Y. Crowell Company, New York, 1977.

A Time To Keep. Written and illustrated by Tasha Tudor. Rand McNally & Co., Chicago, 1977.

Tasha Tudor's Bedtime Book. Kate Klimo, ed. Platt and Munk Publishers, New York, 1977.

A Tasha Tudor Sampler. Written and illustrated by Tasha Tudor. David McKay, New York, 1977.

Carrie's Gift by Efner Tudor Holmes. Illustrated by Tasha Tudor. Published by Wm. Collins-World (Now William Collins Publishers, Inc.), New York, Cleveland, 1978.

An Advent Calendar. Written and illustrated by Tasha Tudor. Rand McNally & Co., Chicago, 1978.

Tasha Tudor's Favorite Christmas Carols. Written and illustrated by Tasha Tudor with Linda Allen. David McKay, New York, 1978.

A Book of Christmas. Written and illustrated by Tasha Tudor. William Collins Publishers, Inc., New York, Cleveland, 1979.

Tasha Tudor's Old-Fashioned Christmas Gifts. Written and illustrated by Tasha Tudor with Linda Allen. David McKay, New York, 1979.

Springs of Joy. By Tasha Tudor et alia, illustrated by Tasha Tudor. Rand McNally & Co., 1979.

Starling Burgess (Tasha Tudor) with her beloved Scottish nanny, Mary D. Burnett.

I

Earliest Years

The roots of my mother Tasha Tudor's character are planted deep in the New England countryside, from which she has drawn the inspiration for her books and paintings. Her family background also undoubtedly helped to form her personality and nurture her many unique talents. Like my mother, her parents were strong-minded individuals who enjoyed rather different and unconventional lifestyles. Her father, my grandfather William Starling Burgess, was known to all as "the Skipper," as he was a noted yacht designer and an enthusiastic sailor. He was born on Christmas Day 1878.

Her mother, the accomplished portrait painter Rosamond Tudor, was born in June 1877. She always used her maiden name professionally. The only memories I have of my grandparents were given to me by my mother, as they both died when I was very young. But my mother portrayed their vital and stimulating personalities so well that my brothers and sister and I have the feeling we knew them to some extent.

My mother, Tasha Tudor, was born in Boston in August 1915. Her oldest brother, Frederic, was then nine years old. Her parents were living in Marblehead, Massachusetts. Her

father, the Skipper, was a man of many skills and interests. He had an airplane factory on the property, where he designed and built small planes. He was also extremely fond of fantasy. He often told my mother wonderful stories and sometimes dressed up as a pirate or some other romantic character from the tales. He was extremely gifted at reading out loud, especially poetry which he occasionally wrote himself.

My mother was christened Starling Burgess, after her father's family. The name was chosen by my grandmother, but the Skipper did not care for it. He was very fond of Natasha, the heroine of Tolstoy's *War and Peace*, and thought this would be the perfect name for my mother. So one day he and my uncle Frederic rechristened her on the back porch over a bottle of wine. Apparently her mother had no choice in the matter, and the name remained for good, eventually shortened simply to Tasha.

William Starling Burgess ("the Skipper"), Tasha's father, at the tiller of a small sailboat. A well-known naval architect, he was an avid sailor.

Rosamond Tudor, Tasha's mother, was an accomplished portrait artist. She used her own name professionally, anticipating the current feminist practice. Tasha, christened Starling Burgess, chose to use her mother's family surname also.

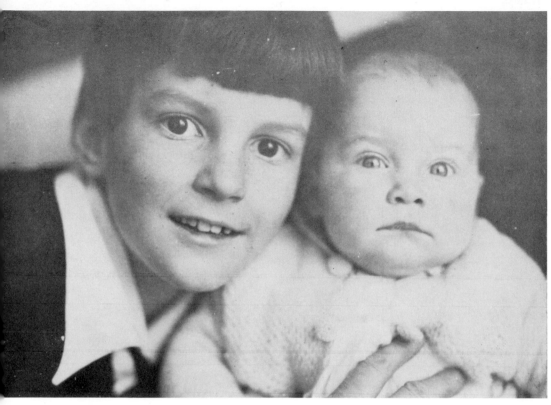

Tasha as an infant, with Frederic, her elder brother.

Though generally favoring "the Bohemian life" of an artist, Tasha's mother also enjoyed the social graces of "proper Bostonian" living.

Although both Grangrin (as my grandmother was called by us) and the Skipper were nonconformists in many ways, they had impeccable manners and all of the social graces. Tasha Tudor is much like her parents in these respects. She, too, has chosen to live by her own standards rather than those ready-made by society. The result has been a most interesting and successful way of life. Rosamond Tudor was an artist, too, but she was interested primarily in the fine arts and portrait painting. She attended the Boston Museum School of Fine Arts and later continued her training under several prominent artists.

Of course growing up in such an artistic atmosphere helped bring out my mother's latent skills. However, unlike her mother, she did not want to be a portrait painter, but an illustrator only. Even as a child, she loved to draw people in the costumes and settings of past centuries. Both her parents were very intellectual, especially Grangrin, who was extremely well read, and saw to it that the young Tasha was exposed early and often to the best literature.

From the time my mother was born until she was nine, she and her parents lived in or near Marblehead, Massachusetts. She had a beloved Scotch nanny, Mary D. Burnett, whom she called Dady. Dady was a second mother to her and kept in close touch with her for many years, even after Tasha's marriage. My mother adored Dady. Many were the times when Dady would sing wonderful Scotch ballads to her, which my mother still remembers. Being very domestic, she helped my mother learn the "womanly arts" of cooking, sewing, and housekeeping at a very early age. Of course Grangrin did this, too, when she wasn't painting. When my

The Skipper, a gifted storyteller, receives an impromptu decoration from his daughter, an enchanted listener.

Baby Natasha (the name was later shortened to Tasha) with "Dady" (Mary D. Burnett). Dady remained with the family for many years.

BY GEORGE S. HUDSON

ESSEX, March 25 — A shrewd east wind goose-quilled the legs of a pair of pipers who topped off a launching here today. It flapped their kilts, too.

She is a yacht, the 70-foot waterline auxiliary Argyll, owned by Lamont Dominick, New York banker, who admits lure of the South Sea isles. Although the bagpipes fitted into the exercises admirably, real old Scotch was missing. Mr. Dominick frankly stated the Scotch would better be kept, and therefore substituted wine of rare vintage in a container the like of which this township never saw before.

Miss Natasha Burgess, 8, daughter of W. Starling Burgess, naval architect, was the Argyll's sponsor. One arm held a spray of roses, the other smashed the wine against the port bow as the yacht slid down the ways of A. D. Story's yard, making a total of 342 vessels he has built.

Tasha Tudor relishes gala spectacles and colorful celebrations, a taste possibly formed by participating in such events as this ceremonious yacht launching.

THE BOSTON HERALD, WEDNESDAY, MARCH 26, 19

GIRL CHRISTENS YACHT ARGYLL

Miss Natasha Burgess, 8-Year-Old Daughter of W. Starling Burgess, Naval Architect, Who Acted as Sponsor at Launching of Yacht.

East Wind Nips Legs of Pipers As Beauty Yacht Is Launched

A portrait of her brother Frederic painted by
their mother is a favorite possession.

mother was a bit older, all three of them sometimes took turns cooking for each other.

At times my mother led a very formal life when her mother took her to live in Boston. There would be maids and servants, and little girls' parties, to which she was escorted by Dady. There were dancing classes, too—she remembers being driven to these by an old Irish coachman in a horse-drawn carriage. The streets of Boston were all cobblestone then. My mother did not much care for this formal life and longed to get back to the country.

Even as a child, Tasha loved animals and country living.

2

A New Kind of Life

Tasha Tudor's parents were divorced when she was nine years old. Her mother went to live in Greenwich Village in New York City, to work seriously on her painting. "The Village" was then a mecca for many important writers and artists, who came there to lead "the Bohemian life." It was a stimulating place for them but not for a child, so my mother was sent to live with family friends in Redding, Connecticut.

"I was dumped into the most unconventional atmosphere you can imagine. It was the best thing that ever happened to me." That is how my mother describes her feelings about this sudden change in her life. "We lived on practically nothing but rice and tomatoes, cold cereals and quickly put-together meals, as Aunt Gwen was far too wrapped up in writing plays to have time for elaborate cooking, yet she often read out loud to us at night — sometimes until ten or eleven o'clock!"

In costume, with best friend Rose. Tasha was even then strongly drawn to the theater.

"Aunt Gwen," close family friend with whom she lived for several winters, opened up new dimensions of creativity for the young Tasha.

Rose — Aunt Gwen's daughter — was a little older than my mother, but they became close friends, along with three other girls who lived nearby. The five creative, imaginative girls had wonderful times together. They spent much time roaming through the beautiful Connecticut countryside. Rose lived then (and still does today) in an old house that was surrounded by green woods and lovely fields filled with wild flowers. It was here that my mother and the girls enjoyed one of their favorite pastimes, known as "being people." Together they acted out characters from the wonderful romantic books read aloud at night by Aunt Gwen, whom my mother adored. Such books as *Carmen, The Cloister and the Hearth,* and the works of Dumas and Shakespeare were a few of the inspirations. My mother, who was very feminine with long blonde hair, always played the part of a young girl or lovely princess. This worked out perfectly as the four others usually wanted the boys' roles anyway. The girls had a secret club called the PSO. Nobody every told what the letters meant, despite the fact that they were teased by various male cousins; it remains a secret to this day. The club members had many interesting experiences and much to discuss amongst themselves! All the girls were highly imaginative. My mother found her new life exhilarating after her rather strict and formal life of little girls' tea parties, in starched dresses and Boston apartments, well supervised by grown-ups. Here in Connecticut she could run wild in a state of utter relaxation from discipline. Nothing was ever on schedule at Aunt Gwen's house, except on weekends when Rose's father came home from his job in the city. This was an occasion of great merrymaking. Uncle Michael, as he was known to my mother, always brought a large roast of beef, along with candy and oranges for the children, and Aunt

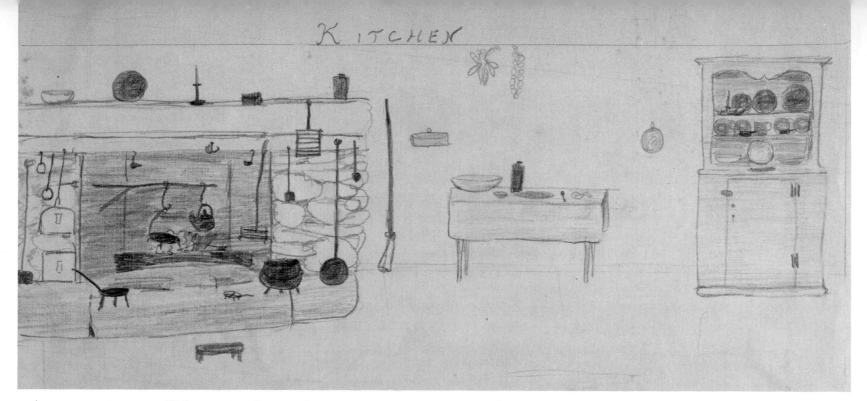

As young as nine or ten, Tasha spent much time at her art. This early sketch shows her fascination with the authentic detail as well as the charm of early American furniture and household objects.

Gwen cooked up special meals. Everybody had a wonderful time.

My mother was very much interested in dancing and the theater. She and Rose and the other girls often acted out cleverly written plays by Aunt Gwen. "They were really wonderful and quite professional," my mother comments. These plays were given in a neighbor's garage. Several professional artist friends volunteered to help with painting the scenery, which raised it above the usual amateur level. Tickets were readily sold to these plays, and they became very popular in the neighborhood. Before each play, my mother gave a small dance performance. She was very gifted

at this and nearly chose to make a career of the dance, instead of art, but finally decided that the life of an artist was more appealing. She had by this time become extremely fond of nature and the country, and she did not like the idea of training and working with dance in the very different atmosphere of the city. So she chose to become an illustrator and a country woman.

Tasha Tudor's schooling was not of the usual sort, yet she is deeply educated and widely read. She says, "I didn't start school until the age of seven, and I never got past the eighth grade. I didn't pass a single test and spent most of the time decorating my copybooks. I hated every minute of school, except the few years with Uncle Henry." While living with Rose and Aunt Gwen, my mother and the girls went to school at Uncle Henry's house from nine until twelve only. The rest of their time was free. But Uncle Henry was a very inspiring and wonderful teacher. He was interesting and amusing. My mother recalls his highly original method of punishing those who did not pay strict attention to their lessons. They were sent into a closet where hung "the skunk coat." This garment acquired its name from the night that Uncle Henry stroked what he thought was a kitty; the disaster is described in Tasha Tudor's book *Snow Before Christmas*. After an interval in the closet, everyone could tell that you had been naughty—by the smell. My mother feels that the only worthwhile education she received was obtained through the hours and hours of reading done at Aunt Gwen's and the brief period of Uncle Henry's training.

Her own experience at "Uncle Henry's" unconventional but excellent school is fictionally depicted in Tasha Tudor's book Snow Before Christmas (above). *At right is a snapshot of the real Uncle Henry.*

18

Tasha's early notebooks often featured lavishly costumed characters, like this sorceress (right) and flower seller (left).

Tasha with two pupils in Bermuda.

Bethany, a favorite name, was given both to a beloved cow and to Tasha's firstborn daughter!

After enduring a few years at a nearby boarding school, Tasha was through with formal education. (Her age was about fifteen.) Then she and her mother spent quite a few winters in Bermuda, where two aunts lived and offered them a place to stay. "I didn't really enjoy Bermuda very much and couldn't wait to get home to Redding," said my mother. But she spent a successful and productive time in Bermuda. She earned some money by getting up a nursery school all on her own. It was popular and well done, and she had eight small pupils. My mother carefully saved the money she earned with the school as she wanted to buy a cow on her return to the Redding farm, but when she got home, Uncle Rico Tudor surprised her by giving her a cow from his own prize herd of Guernseys, so she was able to keep her well-earned money for other things. Her love for farming was growing, and her new cow made her very happy. It was brought from a farm eight miles away, she had to walk the cow the entire distance back home! The cow's name was Delilah, and later she had a calf whom my mother called Bethany. My mother always loved that name and said then that if she ever had a daughter, she would name her Bethany—and here I am writing this!

Surprisingly enough, my mother says that her love for farming actually began in New York City. She often used to spend weekends with her mother in Greenwich Village, near Bleecker Street. At that time, the one thing she wanted to do was to attend plays, so for two days and nights they would go to a matinée and evening performances at various theaters. They always had a wonderful time. During one visit, a truck loaded with crates of live chickens destined for the market had a slight accident on a street near Grangrin's apartment. Several of the hens escaped from a broken crate. All were caught but one, which was picked up by a neighbor who was a friend of Grangrin's. She saved the pretty white hen and gave it to my mother, who named her new pet Nettie and was allowed to keep her in the apartment. Every day Nettie laid an egg. My mother carried her back and forth from Redding to New York in a small traveling case made for dogs. "I just loved that hen. She certainly kindled my desire for farm life." Unfortunately both the cow and the hen had to be boarded during the subsequent winter that my mother spent in Bermuda. She missed them terribly, but as compensation she drew and painted illustrations depicting lovely farm scenes, already showing the direction her future work would take.

One hen led to another, and Tasha soon had a flock of chickens.

Teen-aged Tasha worked hard to earn the money to buy a cow. Acquiring Delilah was a first step toward the farm she was dreaming of owning.

21

Then, of course, she did a lot of drawing during the summer. She loved to paint wild flowers. In her late teens she set herself the task of painting all the Connecticut wild flowers she could find. This project took her quite a few summers to complete, but she enjoyed searching for plants throughout the lovely fields and woods.

Drawing and painting were now primary and pleasurable pursuits. Shown here are pages from a portfolio of carefully researched paintings of New England wild flowers.

During my mother's teen years, her summers were spent on Grangrin's farm in Redding, winters in Bermuda, teaching nursery school. In Redding, even though she no longer lived with Rose's family, she still performed in plays with her and the other girls. They had many good times together — went to movies, visited at each other's houses, and went to plays in New York. Every year they went to the nearby Danbury Fair. This inspired one of Tasha Tudor's early books — *The County Fair*. At the fair they saw wonderful ox teams along with all kinds of fascinating exhibits. My mother displayed her homemade bread and won first prize. She was very proud of that!

In her mother's rustic Connecticut farm home, Tasha was able to add some geese to her growing roster of pets and farm animals.

23

Tasha examines a blossom she will draw.

Her mother's home in Redding, Connecticut, where Tasha spent her teen years.

Tasha at the age of fifteen.

Sewing and reading have been sources of pleasure throughout Tasha Tudor's life.

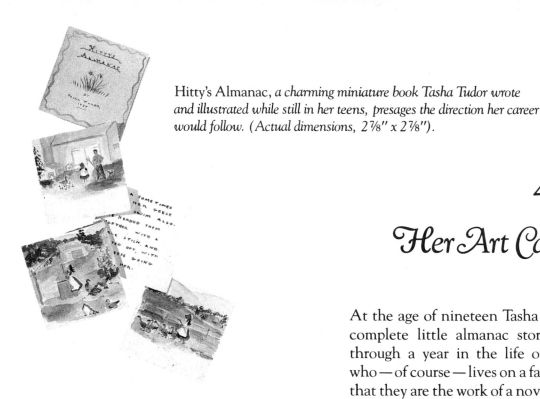

Hitty's Almanac, *a charming miniature book Tasha Tudor wrote and illustrated while still in her teens, presages the direction her career would follow. (Actual dimensions, 2⅞" x 2⅞").*

4

Her Art Career Begins

At the age of nineteen Tasha Tudor wrote and illustrated a complete little almanac storybook. It carries the reader through a year in the life of a young girl, Hitty Fillow, who — of course — lives on a farm. Though the pictures show that they are the work of a novice, my mother's latent skill as an illustrator is very obvious. After passing through the hands of several other people, this special book came into my possession, where it is kept among my treasures. It has never been published as my mother created it just for her own pleasure.

She says that she had already decided upon illustrating as a career when she was quite a bit younger. One day her mother gave her a copy of *The Vicar of Wakefield* with Hugh Thompson's illustrations. "I just loved Hugh Thompson's work, and right then and there decided, I would be an illustrator!" My mother was not particularly fond of writing, but in order to have something to illustrate, she began to write little stories for children, often based on real incidents she had observed.

In 1936 she met my father. He lived in a lovely old house, also in Redding. Although he liked the country to some extent, he was a suburbanite at heart. My mother believed she could eventually "turn him into a farmer." Of course he wanted to please her, and attempted that way of life once they were married, but he did not succeed entirely. My father had a little niece, Sylvie Ann, of whom my mother saw a good deal. In 1938 she wrote and illustrated a little storybook for her called *Pumpkin Moonshine*. Sylvie herself is the leading character in the story, and this was the first book of my mother's that was accepted for publication, after much perseverance on her part! She first bound the handwritten and delicately illustrated original book herself, and made the cover, decorated with a bit of blue calico. Then she took it all over New York to various publishing houses. All of them turned her down. Determined not to give up, she returned a little later and offered it a second time to the Oxford University Press. There a new editor, Eunice Blake, showed much interest in my mother and her work. My mother says that *Pumpkin Moonshine* was the first book Miss Blake accepted in her new position as editor at Oxford, the beginning of a long and successful collaboration, as well as a friendship. (Three of my own picture books were later published by Eunice Blake at J. B. Lippincott Company, in the 1960's.) My mother was thrilled at having her book accepted. Four more so-called Calico Books were to follow: *Alexander the Gander, Dorcas Porkus, Linsey Woolsey* and *The County Fair*.

In 1938 Tasha Tudor was married at her mother's home in Redding, wearing her great-grandmother's lovely wedding dress. There she and my father lived and farmed for quite a few years. Grangrin let them have her house while she herself was away, painting in Guatemala. My father made a

A page from Pumpkin Moonshine, *Tasha Tudor's first published book. Its heroine, Sylvie was based on a real child.*

real effort at that time to go along with my mother's zeal for farming. They had a lot of cows, geese, ducks, and a flock of hens. My father ran a kind of milk route, selling cream, milk, butter, and eggs to nearby people. My mother had to get up very early to milk all the cows and tend her poultry. My father took on the heavy labor, cleaning out the cows' stalls and chopping wood. It must have been hard for him. He really didn't know much about farming or gardening. Most of his early life had been spent in a New York suburb — Pelham Manor. Unlike my mother, he was not passionately fond of country life. His family's lovely old Connecticut home, where my mother met him, had not been acquired until he was grown.

Mother milked the cows by hand and then washed up the pails and the huge milk separator. It was no simple task! First, water had to be drawn up in a bucket at the well house. Since there was no electricity, the water next had to be heated on the wood stove, which took a long time. It was lucky my mother had so much strength and sturdiness. Along with tending the animals, there was cooking, housecleaning, and a huge vegetable garden to care for in the summer with a vast amount of canning to do for the winter. All this with no running water, electric stove, or fancy refrigerator. My mother really had a lot of work on her hands! There was even more when she became pregnant with me, her first child. Today she looks back and does not see how she managed to do it all. Constant fatigue is no pleasant thing to live with! But she was happy, especially about having a baby and starting a family. She was a very warm and loving mother, despite all the work entailed.

The real Sylvie Ann.

Tasha was a loving mother...

...but life was not always easy.

The New Hampshire House

Even Connecticut did not seem rural enough to my mother. She had always wanted to live in Vermont, but my father felt that this would be much too remote. So they settled on looking for a place in New Hampshire. This was during the Second World War, when my brother Seth and I were the only children. For weeks my father saved up gas from our wartime rationing, so we could go on a house-hunting trip to New Hampshire. The journey was not an unalloyed pleasure. My mother recalls that I was car-sick the whole way; we also got lost several times; and then a violent rain and thunderstorm struck. After many tiring hours of driving around, we suddenly came upon an interesting-looking dirt road lined with maple trees. In a short while, the sun

One had to be an artist or "a bit crazy" to know that this decrepit farmhouse could be made beautiful.

burst forth and at that moment we found ourselves in front of an old farmhouse, decrepit to the point where it seemed to be falling apart. "*This* is the house I want," my mother exclaimed. She now says, recalling the event, "People all thought I was a bit crazy anyhow, but they'd have been surer than ever had they seen the tumbledown house I set my heart on. Luckily my poor mother didn't see what I chose for many years."

We went back the next day to look the house over again, and found a man there, on the point of trying to buy it to turn it into a chicken farm. He said he could not seem to persuade the old man down the road into selling it to him, however. By persistent questioning, my mother got the old man's name, and she and my father went to call on him. It turned out that "Uncle Ed" Gerrish—as he was known—was the grandson of the man who in 1789 had originally built the house. He had strong feelings about the kind of people he wanted to have living there. He liked my parents, and when he heard that they wanted to make the place into a home and farm, he sold the house and 450 acres of woods and fields to them. Needless to say, we were all overjoyed! It was with the royalties from her illustrated edition of *Mother Goose* that my mother purchased the place. It was to be our home from 1945 to 1972.

5

Domestic Life

Detail from a painting for a Christmas card by Tasha Tudor.

One early April day when I was five, a dream came true for my mother, though it took years fully to unfold. Only she had the vision and foresight to realize its potential at that time. After searching around New Hampshire, we had come upon the old farm—sadly unloved but vastly willing to be brought to life again by what it takes to make a house a home.

So now, on that bare though promising day in early spring, the family left Connecticut for Webster, New Hampshire. I recall the final move quite vividly. Piled into the old wooden station wagon were the family, then consisting of four, along with a crate of delicate Canton china, our striped tomcat, Simpkin, and two large gray geese. To my brother Seth and me the trip seemed endless, though everybody enjoyed the frequent stops for picnics and to rest the animals. The geese by no means cared for the ride. It was a difficult trip for all concerned. But we finally reached the narrow dirt road leading to the big old house and barn. Slowly we made our way up the road, which was lined on both sides with large

The "haunted house" as the New Hampshire farmhouse looked when they first moved into it.

maple trees, showing occasional glimpses of open fields beyond. Then, at last, there we were at the house. It was spacious, falling down, and looked not a little haunted. The place had been deserted for many a year. Seth and I had loved the house on sight. My parents had been there a few times since our first view of it to negotiate the purchase and to tidy up a few of its seventeen rooms for reasonably comfortable living.

On that April day when we really moved in, Seth and I ran all over the empty rooms in the excitement of exploration. We found much to feed the imagination, though I suppose it was really just dirt and mess for the family to clean up later. Wind whistling through the cracked walls did not deter us as we examined ancient spider webs and dusty evidence of other inhabitants long gone. But time and much hard work saw the old farmhouse gradually begin to change. It was made warm, alive, and interesting by the touch of my mother's hand, plus sheer determination on her part.

Only a few of the rooms were furnished in the early years.

Under Tasha Tudor's hand the New Hampshire farmhouse was restored to its original beauty and its surrounding gardens and fields were filled with a dazzling array of colorful flowers and luscious fruits and vegetables.

Tasha's family continued to grow!

. . . and with it the work. Laundry was a major task without running water or a washing machine.

But what cozy and tastefully arranged rooms they were, even though the house lacked electricity and running water, and had no heat other than wood stoves. It seemed as if our life centered mostly around the big old kitchen with its huge black stove and shining copper pots. Herbs and red-flowering geraniums dominated most of the boxes on the windowsills. It was here in the kitchen that my mother worked long hours on her illustrations and writing.

As children we seldom perceived my mother's tiredness from the demands this life made on her both physically and mentally. That was kept private. But she taught us early to assist her. And despite her appearance of fragility, she was indomitable of spirit and naturally cheerful. Over the years

Though busy with her family and housework, Tasha worked constantly at her art. Her children made fine subjects as these sketches of son Seth show.

the family enlarged until I had another brother and a sister — Tom and Efner. We enjoyed our lifestyle very much. This is not to say that daily living was easy and pleasurable at all times, but my mother presented us with a happy and optimistic light which could not help but have its influence. Children need to grow up surrounded by love, and my mother had much of that to give. Busy as she was, she found time to enrich our lives. I do not recall that there was ever a dull moment!

Though hard work and determination can do wonders, there certainly wasn't enough ready cash to support the family in a style of ease. I never cease to wonder how my mother performed so many tasks in those early years. Many were the hand-smocked dresses and pretty homemade skirts that Efner and I wore as we grew up. Handknit sweaters, socks, and mittens were also enjoyed by everybody. Not all of these were made by my mother, however; many of them came from a loving grandmother in Connecticut. Nevertheless, my mother could do the impossible, it seemed. A great deal of her life centered around us children, but she also needed much time and inspiration for her painting and writing.

My most vivid memories of my mother in those early New Hampshire years are related to her art. Many were the happy hours we spent with her in the big farmhouse kitchen. At an old-fashioned table by the east window, she would be busily drawing and illustrating. The table was always arrayed with bits of nature collected from field or garden — flowers, berries, and seedpods stuck in a glass, or perhaps a mouse or a frog, captive for a few hours only, in a large glass jar arranged with moss, tiny ferns, and dried grass. I am sure my own passionate love of nature must have been greatly inspired by that wonderful table and my mother's love of beauty.

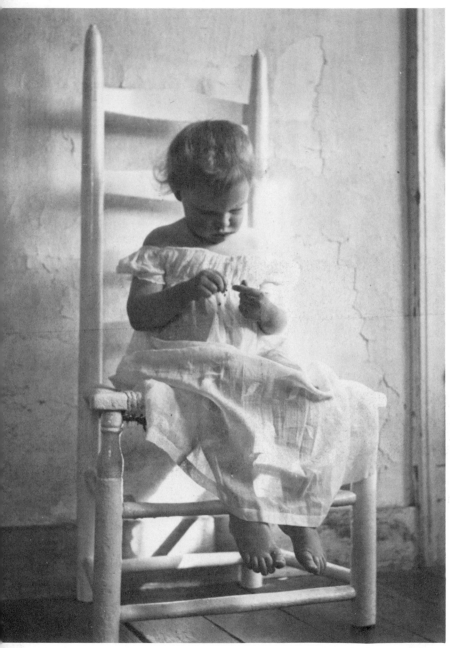

Daughter Bethany was a frequent model. She loved to dress up in antique costumes (left, and on opposite page) and pose. Sometimes too, she would hold an animal for her mother to draw—which would later adorn a greeting card or book. (Above).

People were her favorite subjects to draw, though they were usually people of another century. Often we four children modeled and posed for characters in her stories. That was lots of fun! First, it meant a trip to the attic. From under the eaves were dragged old wooden trunks containing a delightful assortment of antique "dress-ups" of all sizes to fit everyone. The calico dresses were my favorites along with the button boots, which were incredibly narrow. The boys looked fine in gingham shirts with straw hats, perhaps, or trousers buttoning onto little short jackets. But my mother

Bethany and her brother Seth play in antique clothes as their mother sketches them.

Children also had to be fed.

looked the most perfect in those old clothes — she has a face that belongs to another century. Sometimes, after being sketched, we were allowed to keep on the dresses and enjoy an afternoon tea party in the best parlor. We felt as if we were actually living some of the wonderful old fairy tales and stories my mother read to us so constantly.

Reading aloud is a family tradition still enjoyed by all of the family. Here Tasha Tudor as a young mother reads to son Seth and nephew Rico Tudor.

A good deal of my mother's life has been plain hard work, but right along beside that, she has always found time to make us happy. She has taught us certain values through play and work, from which we benefit to this day. Now as a mother myself, I enjoy many of the domestic arts my mother spent hours teaching me in the past.

What happy days we shared in the old kitchen! It usually smelled deliciously of baking bread, spicy cookies, or applesauce. One summer day when I was twelve, my mother said determinedly that it was time I learned to make bread! I had always been encouraged to shape and knead dough for tiny loaves or buns whenever it was bread-making day, but now I must begin from scratch. What time and patience is required to teach a child new skills, when it only takes a minute to finish up neatly yourself! My poor mother. Here I was with dough sticking to my hands and the marble counter, plus flour dusted everywhere. Endless chores awaited my mother, but I was patiently guided—many times, finally to succeed. What a sense of accomplishment one gets, upon admiring a row of well-shaped brown loaves of bread or hot rolls straight from the oven, to delight the family.

For several weeks, one summer, we went through the sponge-cake section of the *Boston Cooking School Cook Book*, trying each and every recipe. Since our chickens always supplied vast quantities of eggs, we went wild with this experiment. Many of the cakes were light and tasty, but sometimes they definitely were not! One chocolate sponge was a total failure—heavy and coarse. My mother took up the cake, rushed out the back door, and sailed it over the chicken-yard fence. Hens rushed from all directions, cackling loudly. Just at that moment some unexpected guests were advancing toward the house. They enjoyed a full view of the henyard, but we were not aware of them. My mother and I were laughing heartily as the rooster sank his beak into

The New Hampshire house was gradually restored and furnished with mellow American antiques.

The wood stove was not chosen for its atmosphere and charm, but for its usefulness. Cooking is regarded as an art and a pleasure, not a chore, by Tasha, and she and all her children are gifted cooks.

Much of the Tudor family life centered about the fireplace, especially in the winter when it and the kitchen stove were the only sources of heat.

Generations of Tudor children have enjoyed the antique rocking horse.

Tasha Tudor's four children, Bethany, Seth, Tom and Efner grew up close to nature in New Hampshire.

In addition to early American specialties, Tasha is proficient in French cuisine.

the cake and invited his hens to partake of the delicacy. I think the visitors were startled by the scene. It was not what they had expected of a famous artist.

It was not only the girls who cooked. Both my brothers were quite accomplished in the kitchen, also. To this day, not even my mother can make chocolate fudge to compare with Seth's or Tom's. But nobody can surpass her in the creation of delicious soups and broths. Maybe it's witchcraft. She has said, "I am proud to claim some Salem ancestry!"

41

Sewing took up quite a bit of my mother's time, but she considered that a pleasure. Most of our clothes she designed and made herself, especially when we were fairly young. Smocked dresses took ages to make, but I had a good many. Summer afternoons in the lawn chairs and winter evenings by the fireside were put to good use. While my mother sewed, one of us would read out loud to her or just play quietly — at times.

Efner and I eventually learned the art of sewing. As children, the four of us had numerous stuffed animals and dolls. From my mother's wonderful piecebag, we could choose all sorts of snippets for a duckling's gown or perhaps a bear's pinafore. Such fun we had designing and cutting! But best of all came the moment when my mother put down her own sewing for a bit. In no time she would fashion a little jacket or skirt for Efner's Mrs. Bear or a stylish hat of straw for my Samantha Duckling. How we treasured those wonderful clothes! It seemed so effortless for my mother, but I guess the secret lay in the fact that her favorite type of sewing was making doll clothes.

Family picnics were frequent events, on the sandy banks of the Black Water River. Tasha usually took her sketch pad and watercolors with her.

Tasha has always loved to sew, and made most of her own and her children's clothes.

*The children often posed
while their mother sketched them.*

Afternoon tea was — and is — a daily institution.

6
Portrait of The Artist

Fond and earliest memories of my mother as an artist lead me
back to a delightful occupation. Afternoon tea was a
pleasurable event which my two brothers, one sister, and I
shared most happily with my mother. Of course there was
always a tempting assortment of homemade treats and China
teas, tastefully served in pretty cups and dishes. But that was
only the beginning.

Depending on the season, our afternoons would frequently be spent drawing, either by the parlor fireplace, or
under the shade of a favorite maple tree overlooking the
flower gardens. Summer always brought many subjects of
interest for my mother to capture in her sketchbooks. Such

Squee

Madame Piggy Pig going to market

Mr. Squee facing the deplorable facts of his family vegetable bill.

Animals, too, were favorite subjects.
A pair of pet guinea pigs are sketched realistically,
then fancifully anthropomorphized for the
family's amusement.

Even the cat enjoys posing.

45

"SHOOH, SHOOH! YOU NAUGHTY GANDER", SAID SYLVIE, AND SHE HAD TO FLAP HER PINAFORE AT HIM BEFORE HE WOULD LEAVE THE FENCE AND COME WALKING.

Life imitates art. Above is a page from Alexander the Gander, *one of Tasha Tudor's early "Calico" books (so named because they are bound in calico-patterned cloth). At right, Bethany feeds the original Alexander and Araminta.*

delightful afternoons we spent together. Working in pencil, my mother would first encourage and help us as we drew pet rabbits, chicks, ducklings, wild life or anything else that was pleasing to the eye. I never ceased to enjoy the pleasure of watching the skill with which my mother caught the close detail of her subjects. Many of these sketches were put to good use over the years in her various illustrated stories.

Sketching was not limited to the house and farm. There were often trips to nearby villages or other places of attraction for my mother to draw. Some of us usually accompanied her, and we made a special day of the excursion. Lovely picnic spots were never hard to come by, especially along the dirt roads we used to find. Not infrequently we visited a favorite antique shop or two. My mother has always been intensely interested in the old ways and everything to do with them.

In occasional villages she would stop to draw the graceful and simple lines of an old New England church or maybe a picturesque house and barn. Later these sketches would be woven into illustrations or Christmas cards showing the same scenes inhabited by people of another century. My mother has a wide collection of antique clothes for adults and children, which we loved to model. She herself says she feels more at home in long dresses, so nearly all her life she has worn skirts that are not exactly within the realm of today's style, but which have a classical grace and charm.

Sketches of nearby villages often appeared on Tasha's popular Christmas cards.

Late fall and winter afternoons were quite different from those of summer, but equally as pleasurable. Hot tea or cocoa by the open fire was just part of every day, when chill winter kept us all inside together. The hours we were in school were the best times for my mother to plan and create her books and Christmas cards. Many hours she spent at the kitchen table, which has always been her desk of profession. Here she could tend a small child or do necessary cooking on the black wood stove, in between drawing. She always claimed it made work much pleasanter to vary it with other occupations. You never had to sit a great length of time at one form of work.

We lived and worked in the old New Hampshire house for many years. My mother's art shows very strongly the influence of our lifestyle. I feel the complete authenticity of her work is one of its greatest charms. It is not difficult to sense my mother's love of beauty and of nature in all her work. The four of us children grew up enriched by her self-determination and ever-flowing spring of inner resources. Times were not always easy during the period of my early recollections. Looking back now, I can fully appreciate my mother's strength of character and her tremendous will to succeed.

Bethany and Efner posing for The Dolls' Christmas.

48

Vegetables and flowers are mixed in rich and colorful profusion. Tasha, barefoot, steps over a giant cabbage to reach a perfect flower for the large bouquet she is preparing.

7

Farming in New Hampshire

We all enjoyed the farm together. My mother often said she wanted to live a life similar to that of New Englanders in the past century. So that is what our family did, in a way, for many a year. It was not easy, but the rewards were most satisfying. One could say my mother's whole art career has been inspired by her lifestyle, plus the farm pets and animals. It all came about gradually, over a long period of years.

Now that we owned the wonderful farmhouse and large barn, it was not long before we acquired a Jersey cow — Mrs.

A sign on the barn door proclaimed: "New Hampshire Farm Bureau Member." The farm was a real working farm, not just a showplace.

Tasha's busy day included feeding Beauty and her colt, Tully.

Tom with Edgar Allen Crow and another pet crow.

Mocha—and some chickens. Every animal on the place immediately became a beloved pet, and possessed great character. Each of us four children always had some kind of small pet, such as a rabbit, guinea pig, or duck, but of them all, Mrs. Mocha commanded the most respect. Much that the family loved centered around the cow. Her delicious milk and her thick yellow cream, we enjoyed daily. Trips to the barn were a delight to the senses. Long, sweet-smelling hay was always there for us to play in, after pulling some out for Mrs. Mocha's breakfast or supper. If we tired of the hay loft, it was always fun to watch my mother milking or to try to do it ourselves. Close by would be an assortment of friendly barn cats or a Corgi dog or two, waiting for their share of the warm milk.

After breakfast the milk was set in jars in the cool pantry, in order for the cream to rise to the top. Once a week my

The fresh butter has been washed and kneaded with a wooden paddle to remove last traces of buttermilk and air bubbles. Now Tasha is patting it onto a wooden butter mold.

mother would get out the old-fashioned crockery butter churn and pour in the thick cream she had saved up. When it was the correct temperature, we would all take turns at working the wooden dasher up and down. It seemed ages before little golden pieces of butter would form, but when it was finally just right, my mother poured off the buttermilk and rinsed the butter in clear cold water. This she did in a large wooden salad bowl with a handmade butter paddle. Then came the best part—printing the butter. Arrayed on one of the pantry shelves were the beautifully carved wooden butter molds, in many shapes and designs. My favorites were acorns-and-oak-leaf, thistle blossom, strawberries, a swan on ripples of water, and a cow grazing beneath a flowing design of wheat and grasses. It was wonderful to watch my mother deftly pack butter into one of these molds, then press it down and pull off the mold. There on a blue Canton china plate would be a sight we never tired of admiring. We could hardly bear to cut into the beautiful cow or swan when butter was served.

Now the butter is ready for use, charmingly imprinted in various patterns.

51

Bethany kept a flock of geese outdoors . . . and ducklings indoors!

When there was extra milk in the springtime, my mother often made cottage cheese and sometimes cheddar. In the warm beautiful month of June, Mrs. Mocha usually presented us with a tiny calf. It would be the color of coffee and cream, with large eyes and tremendous appeal. The four of us would play with the calf when it was old enough to run around a lot. It was as much fun as a big puppy and just as playful. Mrs. Mocha gave quantities of milk then, so my mother enjoyed making a lot of cheese and butter, along with delicious custards and puddings.

As far back as I can remember, we always had a flock of lovely brown hens and a fine rooster with bright comb and wattles. Waking to his early morning crowing was one of the great pleasures of farm life — at least, for me. Our flock usually consisted of about twenty, and they were allowed complete freedom of the barnyard and the fields beyond. As a result we never lacked for large and wonderful-tasting eggs. In the pantry there was always a large antique yellow crockery bowl filled with them. A cook's delight! My mother did not think twice about mixing up an eight-egg sponge cake whenever she felt we needed a treat. Sometimes there would be doll-sized cakes for us to eat for mid-morning snacks, which we called "elevenishes." My mother was always making life extra-pleasant for us in little ways. In warm weather we would sometimes sit out on the lawn with fruit punch and tiny cakes for a mid-morning break. Soon, along would come the corgis and cats, knowing full well they were to share a bite, too. I usually had pet goslings, who were not supposed to be on the lawn but were. They knew how much I loved them and would sit next to me, nibbling grass and accepting cake crumbs with relish. Those pauses in the day with the animals and little treats were part of what made life most enjoyable. My mother certainly knew how to do this, and carries it on still. My daughter can attest to that!

Gardening

For us, vegetable and flower gardening really began in January and February when the seed catalogs arrived in the mail. On cold winter evenings the wind might be blustering about the old farmhouse, but we did not heed it. Our minds were wandering deep in the pages of flowers and vegetables. My mother always ordered a quantity of vegetable seeds for the summer crop, but it was in the flower section that she lost herself to plans for an even prettier and sweeter-scented garden!

After mentally savoring the delights of corn on the cob, crisp lettuce, peas, tomatoes, and many more, the four of us helped decide what seeds to order. By the old kerosene lamp, my mother sat, neatly printing out the double-paged list. How eagerly we anticipated the box of seeds, which would not arrive until March. This seemed ages away, as we huddled close to the big wood stove.

But, as always, March finally did arrive. Spring rains and sun would begin to waken everything outdoors. We four children spent many a happy hour splashing about in rubber boots, while high in the mist-enshrouded trees the red-winged blackbirds and starlings were voicing their joy. One day the mail would bring that exciting seed box! Into the house we ran with it. There my mother would pause from her baking or drawing to share in the moment of delight. We took turns pulling forth the brightly colored packets of vegetable and flower seeds—a bountiful array of tempting prospects for the summer. The weeding, hoeing, and hard work that would be entailed never entered our heads. It did not escape my mother's though. I am sure she quite clearly envisioned what was to come—first, the sprouting of seeds in boxes on the windowsill; then, later on, planting them out in flats, plus all the other care and time that would be required. But she loved it. Horticulture is just about her favorite pastime, and she has almost a professional proficiency at it.

Weeding and hoeing were definitely our tasks in the summer. And why not? My mother firmly believed that children should not be idle. We received much guidance toward purposeful and constructive work. And it was really quite enjoyable to weed the garden, at least for me. But the seeds came in March, and summer was still ages away, it seemed.

New England springs are slow to warm up, but by late April and early May the soil would be ready for the sowing of a few vegetable seeds. Peas were the first. My mother firmly believes in planting by the phases of the moon. So when it was exactly the right time, we would help hoe the little trenches and drop in the round dry peas. How good it felt to be working outdoors in the thin spring sunshine! Beyond the garden, signs of spring greeted the eye wherever one turned. There were always daffodils in profusion. A joyful, satisfied feeling pervaded us as we dug in the earth and put the seeds into the ground to grow.

Spring melted pleasantly into summer. All the seeds had been planted by then and were beginning to show signs of vigorous growth. We children watched our pumpkin plants

Tasha's life is centered around her gardens in the summer.

daily! It was always fun to see just how large a pumpkin we could produce for Halloween time. Our constant attention must have had something to do with the vast sizes those pumpkins reached. One of Tom's grew to weigh over one hundred pounds. We really had a wonderful time with the vegetables.

But it was the flowers for my mother! My all-time summer image of her would be in the midst of a vast sea of annuals and perennials, cutting or weeding. The aproach to this scene would reveal a devoted corgi valiantly guarding her old shoes and her garden basket. Beyond that, if the weather was particularly warm, my mother would have shed a sweater and frilly petticoat, which could be seen hanging from a rose bush or dwarf apple tree. Then there she would

be, relaxing happily with trowel, gardening shears, and seed packets. Even the weeding was a joy to her. She always found it so pleasant to be amongst the herbs and bright flowers, watching hummingbirds and bees busily feeding, with warm sun making the scene perfect.

Our summer centered largely around the gardens and farm life. A typical day for my mother, when she was not drawing pictures for a book, would be spent in the flower garden. Mornings began in the light and airy kitchen, with breakfast of fresh strawberries and cream, an omelet with herbs, and blueberry muffins. Then one of us children would do the dishes, in order that none of my mother's precious time for herself be lost. She would gather her garden basket, a favorite trowel, and a cookie and set out.

Sometimes she planned enlargements and new gardens in a notebook, where names of flowering bushes, lilies, bulbs, and perennials were carefully listed and their locations about the place recorded. Or maybe she would just spend the day weeding, or setting out the countless annuals she had started earlier on the windowsills.

Around mid-morning everyone would feel the need for an elevenish. In the kitchen Efner, who is an excellent cook, might have baked a delicious chocolate cake or pan of brownies, even though she was then only seven or so. I would fix a tray of glasses filled with iced tea and mint leaves for everybody, plus a plate of delectables, warm from the oven. Out on the lawn under the old hickory tree, we would all gather. Of course various pets accompanied us. At times we had beloved, yet naughty, tame crows—Edgar Allen Crow being one of them. A great delight for us happened when we had ginger ale, and the crows took a drink. First Edgar pulled out the drinking straw and bit it in half. Next he plunged his beak way into the glass and took a large swallow. The fizz in his crop brought forth a fine reaction. Flapping around as if he were a bit drunk, he was really funny. Edgar loved the drink, but we didn't let him have much, for fear of damaging his health. I had a favorite tame starling who went everywhere with me. Once, while we were relaxing on the lawn, he flew off into the garden, where earlier he had watched my mother planting rows of radish seeds. He uncovered and devoured every one of them! Needless to say, my mother was not pleased, but she loved pets a great deal, too.

My mother usually became so engrossed in the garden that she forgot lunchtime, but we never did. Often we made sandwiches and picnicked in the field or sat in the vegetable garden, eating green peas and young carrots. Summer was an enjoyable and happy time for all of us.

My mother loved seeing our house beautifully decorated with cut flowers. Nearly every room was always graced with several of her carefully arranged bouquets of sweet-scented annuals or bright poppies and delphinium edged with gray artemisias. There were always lots of old-fashioned moss roses, too. We loved and admired those wonderful bouquets so tastefully arranged in stoneware crocks, Canton china bowls, or pewter mugs. We were not the only ones who admired the flowers, however. One day we found my sister's small Shetland pony in the parlor eating a fresh bouquet of poppies and ferns from the best mahogany table. He had walked in the front door, and there around the corner he must have noticed the enticing flowers. We hastily and rather nervously backed him out the door. Luckily, he was very mild and polite about leaving.

Summer afternoons could seem quite endless to a young child, but my mother was always active except for a short afternoon rest. She knew how we loved the Black Water River, which wound through the woods about a quarter of a mile below our house. So just about every warm afternoon she would walk down there with us—crows, cats, and dogs following. A sandy beach provided all kinds of pleasure. We made sand castles and little ponds for minnows, which we caught if we were quick enough. Efner made mud pies. These, the crows sometimes came and ate. My mother said they were the only baby sitters who would eat mud pies!

The river was beautiful. It had a lot of shallow places, a clean sandy bottom, and dark amber-colored water. Of course there were many green frogs, along with water bugs and flowing water grasses, for us to play around. After swimming, my mother sat with her sewing upon the lovely soft grass that grew on the upper bank. Tall ferns and overhanging silver maples made dappled shade for her. Up in the trees, warblers and little sparrows twittered and sang. The river flowed placidly between its banks, which were abundant in beautiful wild plants. The scarlet bloom of the cardinal flower was my favorite. Often my mother brought along her sketchbook with which to capture a woodland scene or to draw one of us playing on the beach with the corgis. After about an hour we were ready for the long walk home, which was uphill the entire way. By the time we reached home, we were definitely ready for some cooling iced tea.

Afternoon tea was a fixture in our day, the year round. Summertime was the best time for tea, however. Running along the edge of the vegetable garden was a long wooden grape trellis on which grew two kinds of delicious grapes — light green Niagaras and purple Concords. In the summer the large leaves would provide shade over our lawn chairs and tables. Of course in the fall there would be the added beauty of long bunches of grapes hanging over our heads. In this arbor the family would gather for a pleasant afternoon tea. My mother made wonderful iced tea flavored with mint and fruit juices. Along with this, there might be crisp cookies or a delicate sponge cake. Corgis and cats were invited to teatime of course! After the long, hot trip back from the river, they loved to cool off under the lawn chairs and wait hopefully for crumbs to drop.

At one end of the arbor was the herb garden, with a goldfish pond in the center. The fish were great pets, too, but it was the dogs and tame crows my mother really loved. The three crows enjoyed our tea hour quite frequently, but they were frightfully naughty at times. They liked to tip over glasses of tea or peck at the cake if we were not watching, but their favorite prank was to go underneath the slatted lawn chairs and jab the bottom of some unsuspecting guest. The results were spectacular, at least in the eyes of us four children. My mother had to do the apologizing and the picking up of spilled tea and cake, not to mention the soothing of the ruffled guest! The antics of our pets and farm animals certainly were inspirations, at times, to my mother's art and writing, but the tea hours were instructive, along with being entertaining and pleasurable. Often my mother would read out loud to us or help us with sketching, or perhaps she would sew and knit with Efner and me.

After tea there would be weeding, and then we would help feed the farm animals.

Corgis

Corgi dogs have appeared in so many of my mother's illustrations that she is often asked how she first became interested in them. In 1957 the family was realizing another of Mother's dreams — visiting England for a year, living mostly in Sussex. During that summer my younger brother, Tom, was being tutored once or twice a week. His teacher owned a Pembrokeshire Welsh corgi which Tom greatly admired and liked. After each lesson, Tom would come home and tell my mother how much he loved corgis and wished he had one. In fact he said he was going to save up his money to buy a puppy. My mother didn't take any of this very seriously, especially since it was about time for us to leave for America. But in true Tudor tradition twelve-year-old Tom never gave up on his dream of acquiring a corgi puppy. So one day he got on his bicycle and rode six miles to Midhurst, the nearest town, to look through the local paper for advertisements of corgis for sale. After much searching, he found the name of the Reverend Mr. Jones in Pembroke-shire, Wales. To this gentleman he wrote asking the price of the puppies, and also saying that he wanted to take one back home with him. The vicar was very much touched by Tom's letter and said there would be a fine puppy available in a few months.

When the rest of the family went home, Tom stayed on for another year, in an English boarding school. My mother more or less forgot the corgi incident, until one day she was startled to hear from Tom that the Reverend Jones had picked out an especially good corgi for him—from among fifty others—and would personally bring it to the London airport if Tom wanted it sent home. Tom had spent all his savings on the puppy. At that point my mother just did not want an extra animal, but being her usual generous self, she agreed. So the puppy was put on a plane destined for Boston, and from there transferred to Concord, New Hampshire. Tom would still not be home for many months, but my mother resigned herself to coping with the puppy until his return. I well remember the hot summer day when we got the call from the Concord airport, to please come immediately to collect a crate from London. Upon arrival we were presented with an English tea chest fitted out with a small screen door. Looking through the screening was one of the sweetest little brown pups I had ever seen. "The minute I saw him I was done for!" my mother related recently. "He became *my* dog from then on. We named him Browns, but he was always known as Mr. B. He started my passion for corgis, which continues to this day."

Unfortunately for Tom when he returned, Mr. B did not harbor particularly warm feelings toward him. My mother was his one and only love. Corgis—at least, my mother's—are very possessive. Tom was even greeted at times by jealous

and threatening growls from Mr. B! His reaction to that did not help matters. My mother was so fond of Mr. B that she wanted to be sure of having some of his future progeny when he grew up. The following year she acquired from a source nearby a little female puppy, known for her entire nineteen years of life as Pups. In time Pups and Mr. B produced some beautiful offspring. The prettiest and most winning of them

Favorite corgi Megan wears a daisy wreath at her birthday party.

The dogs enjoy a birthday picnic. The last crumb of the "cake" is savored.

all was Megan. My mother just adored her. Later Megan had an unusually small daughter—Gingersnap—on whom my mother also doted.

Every year my mother gave birthday parties for her favorite dogs. Megan's birthday was in June, and her party was held down on the beach at the river. One year she seemed to know it was going to be a special day, so she readied herself for the occasion. About an hour before the party she disappeared. She showed up a bit later. We found her sitting in the rose garden, surrounded by baby's breath and other delicate flowers, but woe to our sense of smell! Her idea of perfume had been to roll in the smelliest and most undesirable objects to be found in woods or barnyard. Needless to say, my mother had to apply the hose and scrub brush to her before we could start the party.

The birthday cake usually consisted of raw hamburger lightly frosted and topped with flowers and candles. Favors consisted of little paper cups containing dog biscuits. My mother always took pictures of the party but had to be quick at catching the action of the dogs at table—where they were allowed complete freedom. Cake would go in one or two gulps, biscuits were grabbed and spilled, with a good bit of canine quibbling concerning who was to grab the most. Next, over went the improvised table and tablecloth to the great amusement of the onlookers. Then children and dogs jumped into the river to wash off frosting and cool the dogs' tempers. Those parties really were lots of fun for all concerned.

8

Celebrations

Christmas

Long before Christmas, we shared pleasant evenings together making presents and pretty ornaments for the tree. We all felt that presents you made yourself had far more meaning and appeal than those bought hurriedly at a store. My mother always had wonderful ideas for things to make. When we were small, one of our favorites was making decorated boxes. From cardboard, my mother fashioned various small boxes, which she then covered with pretty paper of doll-house-size prints. Then she brought out the stoneware potpourri crock which held delicious dried rose petals, herbs, and spices. Though it was December, the smell

always made me think of summer, when we had picked those roses in the warm sunlight. Into the pretty boxes my mother put some of her special potpourri, then tied each box with a delicate ribbon. A tiny bunch of straw flowers or dried lavender was next added on top, to make the box a very beautiful present indeed!

Cut-paper ornaments and woven Danish hearts were always made at Christmas, along with cornucopias to hold delicious homemade candy. All these things were such fun to make when we were little—and they still are. A lot of our favorite decorations came from Denmark and Sweden. There were straw stars, gold paper mobiles of stars and birds, and decorative forms made from fine, curled wood shavings. A few of these we succeeded in copying. Rye straw stars came out the best.

Early in December we began baking cookies and Christmas cakes. Friends and relations always received a special box of these, so we helped my mother a lot. Those baking days were such fun! My mother would mix up a large batch of

Everyone in the family loved baking cakes, pies and cookies for Christmas.

woodstove, so it wasn't until long after we had gone up to bed that they were done. The cold upstairs smelled deliciously of cake, as we settled down to sleep, soothed by pleasant sounds from my mother still busy in the kitchen.

Sometimes cousins or friends came to stay for the holidays. Then the old farmhouse was lively with children's voices and festivities. On December sixth, St. Nicholas's birthday, we always had a special party. This was held by candlelight in the late afternoon. The day before, we had put up lots of handmade decorations in the large winter kitchen with its wide fireplace. Every year my mother made an Advent wreath to hang over the table. It had four candles, which were lighted, one for each Sunday in Advent. Every year my mother also painted a wonderful Advent calendar, which went up on December sixth. Each day on the calendar had a little door that opened, starting on the sixth and continuing to the day before Christmas. We took turns opening one door each day, and how we anticipated the surprise picture inside. The scenes depicted on these calendars were so beautiful! There might be a village inhabited by corgis, cats, and ducklings, or an animal post office in a large oak tree. Another scene might be a door in the woods with angels descending from a star-strewn sky while people, animals, and dolls sit before the door in expectation.

So on December sixth everyone enjoyed the first hint of Christmas. From then on, the days were filled with wreath-making, decorating more of the house, and finishing last-minute Christmas surprises.

sugar-cookie dough, and then get the basket in which were kept her collection of old tin cookie cutters. Out on the marble counter she rolled the dough; then we were allowed to choose and use the cutters. There were many pleasing shapes, including stars, hearts, and lots of animals and birds. After the cookies were baked, we decorated them with melted chocolate chips. Of course we made many different kinds of cookies, but the only kind of Christmas cake we made was Dundee cake, using an old recipe handed down from a great-grandmother. It took a great deal of stirring and many eggs, along with raisins, currants, and candied cherries. Christmas really seemed near when the house smelled of baking Dundee cakes. They took hours to bake in the black

The St. Nicholas tea party was very much a part of my mother's Christmas tradition. At dusk she would light the first of the Advent wreath candles, along with many others around the room. The candles were made of beeswax and perfumed the room deliciously. They burned longer than regular ones, so we could enjoy them a good while. It was so pleasant to sit by the open fire and admire the pretty decorations around the room. Against one wall the long table was covered with an old-fashioned red tablecloth. Set out upon it would be the blue-and-white Canton china and plates of delicious cookies. On a silver tray, the Dundee cake looked festive with its topping of candied cherries and its pretty design of white almonds. After enjoying tea, everyone gathered around the old melodion and sang carols. Afternoon melted into evening in a happy profusion of talking and present-making. My mother presided over the scene, her favorite cat peacefully purring in her lap, as she sewed or knitted.

After the Christmas Eve doll party, we collected wool socks from the back hall. These were hung in descending order of age along the mantel over the big fireplace. Then my mother or father would read to us from a beautifully illustrated copy of *The Night Before Christmas.* By then, Christmas seemed so wonderfully near! Up to our freezing cold bedrooms we went, anticipating the moment. Warm and happy thoughts soon sent us to sleep.

On Christmas day, my father was up by five thirty to start the six wood stoves, which in the early years before we had a furnace kept our house fairly warm. So we awoke to the clatter of stove lids and the crackling of fires beginning to burn. Downstairs we found lumpy stockings, filled even to the height of the presents on the mantel above. Santa was always very generous to us! As it took nearly half the morn-

Stockings hung on Christmas Eve were opened first on Christmas morning.

ing for the house to heat up, we would all sit together in my parents' spacious four-poster bed, after carefully carrying up the stockings. Then such an opening and exclaiming began! There were so many presents to enjoy, including a few special ones that we had always wanted but never dreamed of owning. Some things came each year—chocolate apples in gold paper, pretty cakes of soap for the girls, candy and cookies that could be eaten before breakfast, and other delights.

After opening our stockings, we hurriedly dressed down by the big stove in the kitchen. My mother began preparing an extra-delicious breakfast, as we set the table and fed the pets. Meals were pleasant occasions as my mother always insisted on using her pretty china and serving tastily cooked food. The long table in the winter kitchen, facing the open fire, was a perfect place to enjoy everything. So, despite the early morning chill, we sat down to Christmas breakfast. After finishing the meal with hot tea, we began the farm and household tasks. The cows had been milked and fed before breakfast, but there was still much work to be done, such as digging out a path through the snow to the barn, or thawing the frozen ice in the water buckets. All this and more took a great deal of time in those early years.

Preparations for Christmas were elaborate. Sometimes we had visiting friends and cousins, and they helped. Very early in the morning the turkey was put to roast in an old-fashioned tin oven before the open fire. We all took turns turning the spit and basting it during the next hours, until it was nicely browned on all sides.

In the early afternoon, the turkey being cooked, we sat down to a long and enjoyable dinner by candlelight and crackling fire. Afterward my mother and father decorated the tree, as we never put it up until just before Christmas. It had to be very fresh, as lighted candles were used on it. Unlike many people, we lit the tree and opened our presents on Christmas night, not in the morning. While the tree was being decorated, we washed up the dishes and then sat down to wait. It seemed ages, but finally the sound of the old family music box was heard, as a "ready" signal for us to come in and see the shining tree! All we could do for a while was to walk around and around it, admiring the candles and many ornaments. Then came the present opening. Such generous friends and relations we had! There always seemed to be an endless number of wonderful presents. Christmas was —and

still is— a very special time for our family. We did not go to church, but my mother conveyed to us its true meaning, through her love, and in her beautiful illustrations on Christmas cards depicting Mother and Child.

Doll Christmas

Every Christmas Eve the doll family also had a tree and presents, including something special for each of us. We had a small folding room that could be set up and decorated for their Christmas. It had pretty wallpaper and a glass chandelier which really lighted. There were also tiny electric lights which went on the tree. Being very fond of her small doll family, my mother spent years collecting furniture and miniature accessories for them. We had a wonderful time setting up a lovely Christmas room. The doll family included Captain and Mrs. Crane and their two children—Thaddeus and Lucy. There were also cousins and aunts. They were very fortunate dolls. Some of the things in their possession included antique furniture, tiny books, a set of minute ivory dominoes, a violin, and a doll-sized crèche. The captain's wife, Melissa, had a collection of miniature bronze and wooden birds and animals. These were always displayed in the Christmas room.

My mother, being inordinately fond of fantasy, made the dolls very much alive to us when we were children. We especially loved their Christmases. Besides the dolls, the four of us played with families of plush ducks and bears. Some of these were always guests at the Cranes' Christmas parties, so we spent much time making cards or tiny gifts. Sometimes when my mother baked, she made gingerbread animals and "thimble" cookies for the dolls. The afternoon before Christmas she spent a long time decorating their tree of spruce twigs tied together. We all sat in the cozy winter kitchen, stringing popcorn and cranberries, eating Christmas candy and making presents, while my mother was lost for a while in her doll world.

On Christmas Eve the dolls opened their presents, and gave us some especially wonderful ones, too. With their tree and the glass chandelier lighted, we sat around enjoying the pretty room my mother had so tastefully set up. Such a lot of tiny presents the dolls received! They had quite a few friends outside the family who sent them gifts also.

The Crèche

Next to the old brick fireplace was an old-fashioned built-in oven. It was rather small and long and very dark. In this, on December sixth, my mother always set up our crèche. Being very clever at making dolls, she had made one year a beautiful Mary and tiny Baby. Over the years several of our toys joined the manger scene. Efner's velvet donkey, along with some wooly lambs, and a plush rooster and hen were just right! There also were rabbits, a charming woolen owl, and some white doves which hovered on thin threads. In no time at all, my mother would set all these things up into a most realistic and attractive crèche scene. A weather-beaten shingle and a few other props gave the effect of a manger. Donkey and lambs stood in some soft hay, peering over the top. In front of this sat Mary in a blue gauze robe, with a gold paper halo against her long hair. With folded wooden hands, she bent lovingly over the Holy Infant. Around His cradle

The doll family celebrates Christmas too. Every year their kitchen and parlour are set up like little stages in which these remarkably lifelike dolls prepare for and enjoy the holiday season. Melissa trims the tree while baby Lucy tells Thaddeus what she hopes Santa will put in her stocking. Their miniature antique furniture has been collected over many years.

63

The crèche set up in the oven of the old fireplace (above) appears on a Christmas card (detail, below).

sat the smaller animals. Tiny doll baskets and spruce tips graced the sides of the brick oven. In front of all stood a pure white candle, which would be lighted only at teatime and Christmas parties.

Birthday Parties

My mother created wonderful birthday parties for us. There were birthdays in the woods for me in summer. These have been well described and depicted in *Becky's Birthday*. At my parties I actually had a beautifully decorated woodland table, with cakes which my mother floated down the river to the party scene — lovely cakes with real flowers on them. One year for a present I received a cardboard doll house in which Samuel and Samantha Duckling lived. Efner had winter birthdays in February, marvelous ones in the best

At Bethany's birthday parties the lighted cake was floated down the river, just as in this illustration from Becky's Birthday.

parlor which would be decorated with plants from the greenhouse and early forced bulbs. As it was very near Valentine's Day my mother always baked a heart-shaped cake. Efner had a family of plush bears and some dolls. For her special birthday presents she usually received clothes or doll-house furniture for them.

Halloween

Every year we grew a fine harvest of large pumpkins for Halloween. Planting the seeds in early June was a job my mother left to one or all of us. We would hoe up large mounds of compost-filled soil in which to plant the flat white seeds, carefully saved from last year's crop. How we anticipated the day when the thick green sprouts would push up through the earth. The plants certainly grew fast! We created a fertilizer for them, which my mother called Rose Jar. She filled a large iron tub with water; then we children went all around the cow pasture collecting dry flops. These were dumped into the water and left to season for a good while. Then the pumpkins were fed with this every few weeks. The vines spread all over the vegetable garden and into the field. It wasn't long before we found many big yellow blossoms. By fall there were some wonderfully large pumpkins. All the small ones had been cut off, in order to let the bigger ones grow to an even greater size. Some weighed over one hundred pounds at harvest.

Making "Pumpkin Moonshines" for Halloween.

Tasha's turkey, cooked in the old-fashioned roaster in the fireplace, is incomparably more delicious than any cooked by more modern methods.

The antique turkey roaster is still in use.

Thanksgiving

Snow flurries and cold winds outside made Thanksgiving in the old house a very warm and pleasant occasion. Friends and cousins usually arrived the day before. What fun we all had! As always, there was lots of work to be done around the farm. So we welcomed extra hands at such tasks as stacking winter stovewood, cleaning the barn, or clearing up the old vegetable garden. Inside, my mother and the other women baked pies and other delicious things for the following day. They were very generous with snacks, when we children ran through the kitchen on our way outdoors.

Sometimes, in late afternoon, everyone would take a walk in the hemlock woods below the house, to hunt for pretty partridge berries, ground pine, and other greens with which to decorate the Thanksgiving table. I loved those walks. Usually the tame crows accompanied us, along with gray cats and several corgis. Beauty surrounded us in the fields and woods, even though the weather was cold. Not a detail missed my mother's observant eye. Dry grasses, a bunch of acorns, or perhaps a lone bird searching for seeds on the leaf-strewn ground—there were endless little things of natural beauty, to be used later in illustrations. After our walk through the woods, we gladly came home to the warm house with all the delicious smells of baking. Despite the fact that my mother was frequently tired at these busy times, she gave much of herself to everyone around her.

Thanksgiving Day seemed long to the four of us children, as dinner was not ready until mid-afternoon. It took many hours for the turkey to roast. Finally my mother pulled it back from the open fire, and we all gathered around, dogs included. Roasted to perfection, the turkey was placed to be carved on a huge Canton platter. At the decorated table, family and friends sat down to a warm and joyful occasion.

Easter

Some of my fondest memories are of Easter when the four of us were small children. The fact that Easter came in the spring, along with the early flowers and birds, made it a wonderfully bright and happy occasion. We spent much time beforehand, decorating eggs or pretty Easter cards. There was always a large Easter egg tree. As it was spring time, the hens were laying quantities of eggs, so were the ducks and geese. A variety of sizes, even to some eggs from my canaries, made the tree more interesting. Decorating the eggs was fun for us all. First we emptied them by blowing out the inside through tiny holes on either end. Some we painted, but the prettiest were decorated by pasting on delicate paper flowers and gold trim. After creating an egg with paper moss roses or forget-me-nots, a delicate ribbon and bow were added. We liked to see who could design the prettiest and most original egg.

The Easter egg tree (detail from an illustration in A Time to Keep*).*

67

*Charming Easter eggs made by
Tasha Tudor and her family.*

On Good Friday my mother always made delicious hot cross buns for tea. We also set up the egg tree, which was a delicate birch sapling just beginning to leaf out. The eggs looked beautiful hung on this! On Easter morning my mother got up before anyone else was awake, and arranged the long winter-kitchen table for a special surprise. Every year she added new pieces to a special set of children's china, on which were designs of dressed-up rabbits doing all kinds of interesting things. We loved this rabbit china, and each of us had our own special dishes and teacups or mugs. How we looked forward to finding new pieces on Easter morning! After my mother had set the table, she decorated it with bouquets of bright tulips and other spring flowers, still fresh with early morning dew. In the center of the table stood the Easter egg tree. Occasionally we were given a much longed-for baby rabbit or guinea pig or some fluffy yellow ducklings. These would be on the table, also, under a large cheese basket. What an unforgettable sight that lovely table was, as we joyfully rushed down to breakfast!

Fourth of July

Through the woods below our house there ran the lovely Black Water River, with its sandy beach. During the summer we swam there almost daily. It was here, too, that we enjoyed many a Fourth of July picnic. The day, which began early, was usually warm and sunny. My mother hung our old thirteen-star flag from the upstairs-hall window. It looked very festive hanging over the big front door.

After breakfast and chores were over, my sister and I helped prepare a large picnic for our day at the river. It had to be especially good, and always included a large watermelon. The food then had to be carried carefully by Seth or Tom down the long woodland path to the river. Not infrequently there were accidents, as such heavy melons had a tendency to slip from the grasp. It was rather embarrassing, especially as the watermelon would usually break into several pieces.

Picnic preparations complete, we packed baskets with food, sketch books, and sometimes our favorite plush animal or doll. Walks to the river were always a delight to the senses. Open fields of daisies and black-eyed Susans were fun to wander through, until we came to the damp, fern-carpeted woods. Then there was a marsh full of frogs, turtles, and other inhabitants for us to discover. Next came the river, flowing over bright clean sand, with the beach above. Under the shade of an enormous old maple, we put down our baskets and set the jar of iced tea in a shallow part of the water, to await lunch.

After much swimming, splashing, and playing in the sand, the four of us would be starved. My mother did not particularly enjoy swimming, so she usually sewed or drew. At lunchtime she spread a red-checked tablecloth upon the soft grass above the beach, and set out our Fourth of July feast. Mosquitoes, sand, and dogs and tame crows were always a part of this occasion, but we loved every minute of it. The crows would dive in and snatch a piece of sandwich, while the dogs hung around for morsels of food which had dropped into a bit of sand.

Valentine's Day

My mother always made much of Valentine's Day for us. Coming as it did at a very cold and wintry time of year, we found the Valentine celebration extremely pleasant. There would be an afternoon-tea party to which our dolls and stuffed animals were also invited. Days ahead of the fourteenth we would get out colored paper, glue, paints, and lace-paper doilies with which to make our valentines. In the evenings by lamp or by candlelight, we would sit together and work. Sometimes we watched my mother paint or cut out pretty hearts. She taught us all kinds of wonderful things. She was especially clever at cutting fine designs in folded paper, which opened out into lovely birds, flowers, and lace. They looked a lot like some of the old valentines, the kind one never sees anymore. She made beautiful hand-painted

Tom and Efner and two friends dress up and pose for a Fourth of July picture book before setting out for the traditional picnic.

Tasha's handmade valentines for family and friends have become treasured keepsakes, like this one, featuring Dr. Cupid Corgi. *The poem is by Tasha, as well as the illustration.*

pictures, too. The doll and animal families always received tiny cards with sentiments and clever verses she made up. Sometimes these arrived at our doll houses by their postal system known as Sparrow Post.

Just off the parlor was a small lean-to greenhouse. It was here that my mother kept many of her favorite sweet-scented flowers. They always seemed to be in bloom on Valentine's Day. Some of these included jasmine, mimosa, climbing roses, scented geraniums, and alyssum. Narcissus and daffodils were just coming into bloom, also. A day before the Valentine party, my mother went with us to a nearby commercial greenhouse just to get a few extra tulips and daffodils in full bloom.

On the fourteenth the parlor was decorated. Flowers graced the room everywhere. In back of the long sofa, where we always sat, was a window that opened wide into the greenhouse, letting in warmth and the scents of the many flowers.

My mother always made a special Valentine's cake, which was baked in a heart-shaped tin. The frosting was flavored with chopped maraschino cherries and juice. This gave it a pretty pink color, and it tasted delicious! At four in the afternoon the doll and animal families arrived in the parlor. They all brought valentines. Captain Crane and his wife and children had a table set up in one corner of the room, decorated with tiny flowers and, of course, a doll tea set and

Even the dolls received handmade valentines, delivered by Sparrow Post! All of these are less than an inch high, exquisitely painted.

Each bunch of flowers can be pulled from its pot, revealing a handwritten message, in this very inventive valentine.

cake. They brought beautiful valentines for the four of us. So we spent a very pleasant afternoon by the fireside, opening valentines and enjoying the springlike atmosphere from all the flowers.

Elaborately hand-cut paper lace valentine.

9

Crafts, Relaxation and Play

The Dolls

My mother has always played with and loved dolls. Her dolls, however, are not ordinary ones, but sixteen-inch tall antique French "fashion dolls," plus a few additional ones that she has made herself. One of her favorite diversions has been designing and sewing clothes for them. This interest began in her early youth. Many were the happy hours she spent as a child, playing with a family of tiny china dolls. Their clothes were lovingly fashioned by her from flower petals; their homes were little stick houses. Everything about them became very real to my mother, through her remarkable gift of fantasy. She played alone a great deal and created her own world. Then, one day in her teens, she acquired Nicey Melinda, a large doll of great character and charm, though much worn by the years. "I just adored Nicey. She was a great solace through the hateful years of boarding school. It was from making clothes for Nicey that I first learned to sew for myself," says my mother.

Then came Sethany Ann, who was much more elegant than Nicey, but lacking in character. Both Sethany and Nicey are described in *The Dolls' Christmas*, a lovely story my mother wrote when I was young.

Today, her favorite dolls are the Captain Crane family, and some attractive cousins. My mother says, "I made Thaddeus Crane myself, as men dolls always look so effeminate. They just look like lady dolls with moustaches pasted on!" Thaddeus is as handsome as Melissa is pretty. As children we all entered wholeheartedly into the fantasy world of the dolls. They seemed real, living people to us, and certainly had very individual personalities. The dolls, our plush ducks, and our bears led very interesting lives.

Doll fairs were annual summer events. It took most of the summer to prepare for them. My mother made little cardboard booths, which I decorated with poster paints. The wares and exhibits were set up in these. Then we worked every evening, "making things" as we called it.

The fancy-work table was one of the most popular because my mother made many wonderful tiny doll-sized items. These could be purchased with buttons as currency. Lots of our friends were invited to attend the fairs with their own dolls and stuffed animals.

The most popular booth of all was the cake booth with

When doll Thaddeus Crane married his Melissa, Life Magazine *came and did a feature story about their wedding.*

Tasha Tudor's dolls have come to seem like real, living people to family and friends.

nearby soda fountain. The cakes on sale there were lovely creations, which we sometimes helped my mother make. There were cupcakes, assorted cookies, tiny lemon pies, and other delicious miniature treats.

Another booth contained flower and vegetable exhibits, with prizes awarded for the most outstanding. We used the tiniest, most doll-sized flowers and vegetables to be found in my mother's garden. This was lots of fun. Sometimes we had art exhibits, and many of our friends contributed doll-sized paintings.

Sparrow Post

The doll's postal system was run by Augustus Sparrow — Postmaster General. Each of us had a cardboard mailbox on our doll house. For many years we kept up a correspondence between our dolls and those belonging to our friends. Tiny letters were written, then delivered by Sparrow Post, which, of course, was another of my mother's inventions. Next, she thought up the idea of having a mail-order catalog so the dolls, ducklings, and bears could purchase ready-made clothes. Mouse Mills was the name of this wonderful firm.

Mouse Mills became so highly successful that a catalog of valentines was created, with the most delightful pictures and

Melissa is a beautiful French fashion doll with an extensive and exquisite wardrobe. Handsome Captain Thaddeus Crane was made by Tasha Tudor. He looks equally dashing in uniform or in his workclothes, as here. All the dolls are astonishingly lifelike.

74

verses imaginable. All our dolls and animals ordered and sent these on Valentine's Day by way of Sparrow Post.

If my mother decides to do something, she will do it. One day she thought it would be fun to make a doll to give to a very appreciative friend as a surprise present. For many evenings she worked, molding the head, sewing a cloth body, and then carving delicate wooden arms and legs. After painting the face very skillfully, she added a handwoven wig of long hair, which could be done up in various pleasing styles. Making the clothes came next. These gave my mother infinite pleasure, as she loved to sew and design dresses, petticoats, and tiny shoes from the styles of about 1860.

Her doll family subscribes to a wonderful magazine known as *The Bouquet* in which is shown some of the latest fashions for dolls. Included is also a social column, some short stories and pictures, children's word games, and more. My mother used to put out a new issue of this magazine four times a year. We loved to read it. The toy animals and dolls were very much a part of our lives when we were growing up.

The Bouquet, *a doll-sized publication created by Tasha Tudor for her children, showed fashionable doll costumes, among other features.*

Mouse Mills *goods could be purchased with buttons in lieu of cash.*

By Sparrow Post *dolls could order valentines, or the latest clothes from* Mouse Mills Catalogue. The Bouquet, *a miniature magazine, also brought stories and news, all of which was avidly read by the Tudor children.*

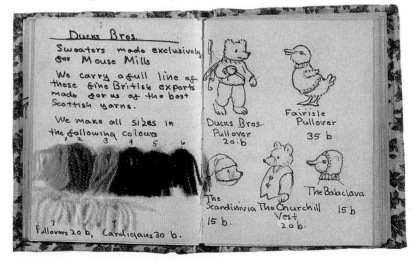

Weaving and Spinning

Ever since she was a small child, Tasha Tudor has been interested in weaving. It was very difficult when she was young to find someone who knew much about it. (Today this is by no means the case, however. Now many books and teachers are available to interested weavers.) But my mother was determined to learn this craft, so much of her weaving skill was necessarily self-taught, or gained from studying a few very old books.

My first memories of my mother's weaving were of watching as she made brightly colored rag rugs for the large kitchen floor. We sometimes helped her with these, too. It was fun to cut the strips of old material and wind them onto the shuttle. Often my mother dyed the pieces to make them a brighter hue. There was every sort of thing for us to get into and tangle, but in the end those rugs certainly looked pretty! At one time the big old loom stood in a corner of the kitchen. It was a very pleasant place for my mother to sit and weave, when she was not busy with other housework. Underneath the loom several striped kittens usually played. The place was irresistible to them, as there were many baskets full of

Tasha Tudor is a skilled weaver.

spools, shuttles, and cloth strips ready to be woven. As tiny childern we played there, also. I believe my mother's patience must have been sorely tried at times, but we were kept happy and busy.

Though the rugs were useful and pretty, my mother really wanted to perfect her skill and make checked or plaid woolen and linen materials, such as the oldtime weavers created. Over the years she figured out most cleverly how to do all these things. She often wears skirts, capes, and shirts made from her own handwoven cloth.

Spinning flax or wool, preparatory to weaving.

These clothes made of Tasha's handspun, handwoven fabrics have a timeless, classic charm.

Spinning flax also interested her. This procedure was learned mainly on her own or with occasional help from friends. She and her mother used to attend many wonderful auctions to buy things for a small antique shop which Grangrin, in addition to all her other activities, ran. On these excursions my mother's love for old things was greatly stimulated. She found most of the implements she needed for spinning at these auctions, then taught herself the art. One

Tasha has an extensive collection of handsome antique dresses, some of which are used for reference in her paintings or illustrations, but many of which she wears herself. Here, she and friends (artist Pamela Sampson, left, and editor Ann Beneduce, with Mrs. Tudor in doorway) model some graceful styles from the mid-nineteenth century.

time when she was in her late teens in Connecticut, she grew a whole field of flax. Then she went through all the procedures required—soaking, retting, cleaning, dyeing—until the flax was ready for spinning. After the threads were spun, she wove material and made a shirt for her brother. It was a beautiful color, and he wore it for years and years. My mother says she was very proud of that shirt. It represented a great deal of work and skill which she followed through from start to finish.

Tasha sculpts and paints delicate miniature scenes inside walnut shells and sends these with favorite poems or quotations on birthdays or other special events.

Basket-weaving in the Shaker manner is another craft in which Tasha delights. Master basket-maker Wayne Rundell supervises as splints are prepared from a black ash tree. Some of her baskets are shown (right).

Boxes are covered in tiny-patterned paper, ribbon-trimmed, and filled with a potpourri of garden flowers to make fragrant gifts for Tasha's friends.

The invitation to the gala premiere performance of The Rose and the Ring *in October, 1978.*

Marionettes

For many years my mother has been intrigued by marionettes. When I was very little, she began creating some of her own, but it was difficult. She had few of the proper tools and practically no informative books on the subject, so she just improvised as she went along. By the time I was about eight, she had created the characters for *Little Red Riding Hood, The Bremen Town Musicians,* and *Hansel and Gretel.* This she did in the evenings, after working hard all day. Next she designed a small portable stage and had it built. My father was excellent at both manipulating the marionettes and at speaking the parts. Seth and I were old enough for this, too. Tom played music between the scenes on an old hand organ. We couldn't help very much in making scenery in the early years, so my mother did this. It was marvelously effective!

Soon we began to give performances—first to interested guests, most of whom were school friends of ours and their parents. As our shows became more and more popular, my mother increased our repertoire and we began traveling—at first just to birthday parties at our friends' houses. Next we were hired by libraries and schools. On these trips Seth and I and Tom were proud to be earning something from the sale of tickets. We eventually traveled as far as the Museum of Natural History in New York City and even all the way to Virginia.

Then there came a great span of years when we gave up the marionettes, probably due to more urgent demands on my mother's time, such as the birth of my sister, Efner. But my mother never stopped thinking about marionettes and collecting interesting and inspiring books about them. In 1965

80

Teaching Bethany to manipulate the marionettes. Performing first for neighbors and friends, the family soon became professionally adept, and gave real (paid) performances in schools, libraries and museums in the early 1950's.

Two of the characters from The Rose and the Ring. *The heads are molded of plastic wood, covered with a thin layer of gesso, and painted realistically. Flexible bodies and jointed limbs are made of cloth and wood. Much artistry goes into the creation of these marionettes. Costumes, too, are handsewn.*

she was greatly excited by a performance in Boston of the famous Salzburg Marionettes. This started a renewed desire to work with her own, but it was not realized until 1977 when she was happily settled in her completed Vermont home. Several times recently she has had the good fortune to see the Salzburg Marionettes perform in their native city in Austria. In 1977, with time her own at last, she set to work in earnest to enjoy and perfect one of her favorite pastimes. A large former goat shed was turned into an attractive place for a stage with room for an audience. With help from talented and interested friends my mother recently created an enchanting performance of William Makepeace Thackeray's story *The Rose and the Ring*. This remarkable performance was totally professional—but shown only to a small, select audience of friends, some of whom had, however, traveled great distances just to see it.

10

A Success Unexpected

*If one advances confidently in the direction of his dreams,
and endeavors to live the life which he has imagined, he will
meet with a success unexpected in common hours.*

— Henry D. Thoreau

In 1971 Tasha Tudor sold the house in New Hampshire.
Sometimes a big change can do wonders for a person. This is
what moving to Vermont did for my mother. Now that we
children were grown and living away from home the
seventeen-room farmhouse was too large and empty for my
mother to live in happily. It was finally the time when she
could realize her dream of nearly thirty years earlier — to live
in Vermont. Her son Seth was already living there in a house
he had built himself. My mother decided to try to find land
fairly close to his, so that he could build her a "new old
house." With her usual good fortune, the first day she went
looking for land in Vermont, she found a good-sized piece for

*(Above) the cozy room in the partially completed "new old house," in
which Tasha spent her first Vermont winter. (Left) A Christmas card
showing the same room, and several of Tasha Tudor's grandchildren.*

82

Tasha Tudor has a flourishing flower garden in front of the new house, in addition to a sizable vegetable garden.

sale adjoining Seth's property. It had a small sloping field; the rest was lovely deep woods, pine and birch. Seth cleared a larger area with his axe and bulldozer. He is a very skilled cabinetmaker and carpenter, so over a period of two years he built the entire house and barn by himself without the aid of power tools. He also made a beautiful, large brick fireplace, including a built-in oven and ash pit at the side. The house is actually a copy of an old one belonging to a close friend of my mother's in New Hampshire. It certainly was a painstaking job for Seth, though very interesting, as he did everything in a manner similar to that of a carpenter working a hundred or more years ago.

Although the house and outbuildings took about two years to complete, the old farmhouse had been sold, and so, as soon as the first barn was up, my mother moved from the New Hampshire farm. There was a great deal to be transported, despite the fact that my sister and I had been given some of the furniture when we left home. Also to be moved were two cows, two ponies, a flock of geese, and the hens. On top of that, my mother did not want to part with her favorite perennials from the garden or her small flowering-crabapple trees. Many were the trips she made from New Hampshire to Vermont with the back of her Land Rover loaded with plants or small trees. Even her valuable, well-rotted manure pile went with her, a few grain sacks filled at at time. She loves her plants! Luckily my brother Tom was available to help with all the digging and loading. Seth was busy building the house and barn.

Seth Tudor, a skilled cabinetmaker and carpenter, built his mother's Vermont house entirely with his own hands. He and his family live nearby.

That first summer in Vermont my mother lived in a horse stall, which was fitted out with cot, bureau, and mosquito netting. I stayed in the New Hampshire house to care for the animals and remaining furniture until the final move. Seth built the barn first, in order to accommodate the animals. Part of the house was to be finished by late fall. By that time, it was pretty cold and there was still a lot of hard work for my mother to do. Her pioneer spirit and strength, however, upheld her through it all.

One rainy cold afternoon she made the final move, Seth driving a van with the cows and horses, and she following in the heavily loaded Land Rover, with four or five corgis included. She says she does not wish ever to recall that day — trying to unload the restless animals in the early Vermont twilight, then getting the wood stove lighted to warm her frozen hands. Next, water had to be hauled from the nearby spring; the animals had to be fed; and only then could she prepare a meal for herself in the makeshift kitchen that was full of unpacked boxes. There was no electricity, of course. That fall was exceptionally cold and raw. I recall in mid-October helping at times to mix heavy loads of mortar while Seth put together a small greenhouse to accommodate my mother's house plants and camellia trees. It certainly was cold! But my mother now had two small rooms of the house that were partially finished in which to spend the winter. These were fixed up cozily with the old cookstove for their only heat. There was also her art table near a window, where my mother would sit, wrapped in a blanket, when she was drawing or writing. Aside from that, her day consisted of cooking, splitting wood, stoking the stove, hauling water, and caring for farm animals, dogs, and three hardy canaries, who sometimes found the water in their drinking cup frozen in the morning. But everything survived until spring.

The frame of the house goes up; a dream takes shape.

Winslow, Seth's son, inspects his father's handiwork.

The siding and roof go on. The house was designed by
Tasha Tudor, based on a very old and very lovely house owned
by a friend and much admired by Tasha.

The house, greenhouse, and barns are complete and snug,
as the cold Vermont winter sets in. It is necessary to be self-sufficient
here as the snow often drifts to depths of five or six feet.

Then my mother rushed into gardening. After the tree stumps were removed, she set to work on the clearing with a Rototiller and turned up a patch for her vegetable seeds. As usual, she had a wonderful garden. Pots of bright petunias around the porch were to be her only flowers that year. There was too much building and driving around of trucks to be done before she could start on her flower beds.

The second year she had a large stone-walled terrace built in front of the house and on the slope below it. There are two levels of gardens there, in which flowers abound. Lilac

By the second year in her new home her famous "green thumb" had produced flowers in joyous abundance.

The barns and house, a composite view. In the large open barn at the far left, the Tudors sometimes hold a square dance for their friends, complete with "caller" and a country fiddler.

bushes and flowering vines adorn one side of the house. Farther out, in front, there are flower beds, crab-apple trees, and, in spring, a field of daffodils. After a few years my mother found that her acreage could not support cows and horses satisfactorily, so she decided to keep goats instead. These do not require grazing land on any large scale, as they prefer to browse on twigs and leaves.

Her corgis loved the Vermont home immediately, as they were allowed to roam freely through woods and fields. In New Hampshire the house was right next to the road, so the dogs usually had to be penned in.

An old-fashioned bonnet protects her from the sun as she works in her garden, her corgi Katey a constant companion.

The corgis love the freedom of their new home.

Her Art and Attainments

Tasha Tudor passionately loves to draw — it has been the center of her whole life, and she finds it extremely satisfying, especially now that she can draw whatever she wants with great skill. She can put down on paper exactly what she visualizes in her mind, with a fluency that is a fairly recent attainment. Her tremendous success, which was built up over many years, is a constant source of inner pride and

Tasha Tudor's many books have won awards and honors, including, in 1971, the Regina Medal of the Catholic Library Association, and her admirers, young and old, are legion. Her primary wellspring of joy is her work and her ever-growing artistic proficiency.

She is a much sought-after speaker, but her public appearances are few, because of demanding work schedules and because she must keep some precious time for her family and to pursue her many wide-ranging interests. Also she explains that it is quite hard to find a baby-sitter for a herd of goats, a garden and six or eight corgis.

Grandchildren live within a short walking distance. Above, left, Bethany's small daughter Laura milks Grandmother's goat. Sometimes she is even allowed to ride on a wether goat with Tasha standing by (above). Left, Tasha with a prize Nubian goat.

Marjorie Tudor, Seth's wife, enjoys sketching, too.

Son Tom likes to lend a hand when he comes home for a visit.

happiness. She is a very happy person and does not find the weight of years burdensome in the least.

It is satisfying to her to know that her life continues to be put to a good, useful, and interesting purpose. Today she is very actively engaged, not only illustrating books but also creating individual drawings and paintings just for pleasure.

Grandson Winslow likes to visit often.

Younger daughter Efner, also a writer, shares an autographing tour with her.

Happy afternoons are spent sketching in the company of family, friends and corgis.

*Four grandchildren on a fallen tree trunk:
Laura, Winslow, Jennie, and Julie.*

*Below, the scene
will become an illustration.*

She is constantly perfecting her work and increasing her mastery of her particular style and medium. A very happy part of her life, too, is devoted to caring for a large flower garden and another one for vegetables. She milks her goats and tends a flock of hens. Of course, there are many corgis in the household, and her favorite tabby cat, Miss Purrvis. Two of her children, as well as several beloved grandchildren, live near at hand.

93

Art remains the center of her life.

A recent card, depicting Laura setting out for school on snowshoes, is a fine example of Tasha Tudor's mature style and technique.

At my mother's lovely home you immediately sense a feeling of peace and serenity. This pleasure is increased when you are in her actual presence. A positive, intelligent and creative person, she makes all who are near her feel a warm glow, sharing her appreciation of the beauty that can still be found in this world. I believe she has found the secret of true happiness.

I come in the little things,
Saith the Lord:
Yea, on the glancing wing
Of eager birds, the softly pattering feet
Of furred and gentle beasts.

I come in the little things,
Saith the Lord:
Not borne on the morning's wings
Of majesty, but I have set My feet
Amidst the delicate and bladed wheat.

I come in the little things,
Saith the Lord. Amen.

EVELYN UNDERHILL

A favorite poem expresses Tasha's reverent appreciation for the manifold beauties of nature, and her special regard for birds and gentle, small creatures.